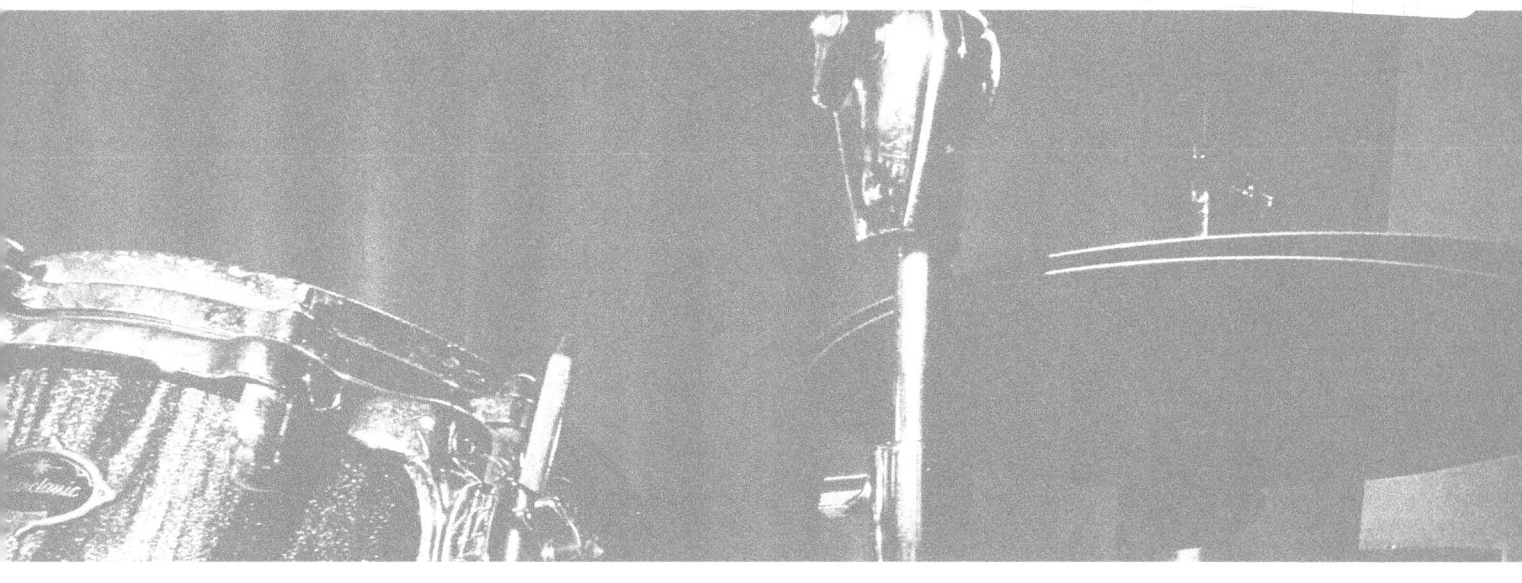

Andrey Pankratov

Kick, Snare, Hat Basics

A Comprehensive Introduction to the Drums for Beginners

All rights reserved at copyright.gov

ISBN: 978-1-962612-22-7

© 2025 Author Andrey Pankratov

Messages about typos, errors, inaccuracies and suggestions for improving the quality are gratefully received at:
avgustaudartseva@gmail.com

CONTENTS

A Note from the Author 5
Hand Placement. Grip 7
Notation. Beat or Measure 9
Time Signatures 11
"Hand to Hand" Technique 13
Kick, Snare, Hat 14
Types of Strokes. Full Stroke 15
Types of Strokes. Moeller Technique... 16
Triplets 19
Playing Single Strokes and Accents.. 20
Rudiments 21
Flam 23
Flam Accent 24

All Videos (Playlist) 25

Short Rolls 26
Pedal Drumming. Playing the Bass Drum 28
Developing Movement Coordination on the Drum Kit 30
Coordination in Triplet Pulsation in Swing Style 34
Linear Coordination 38
Music Styles 41
A Couple More Funk Drawings 46
Brazilian and Afro-Cuban Rhythms.. 47
Train Beat 52
Metronome Lessons 53

List of Recommended Literature 54

A Note from the Author

This book contains a relatively simple, logical method of learning to play the drums. I'd say there are four main areas of basic skill development:
1. Hand technique.
2. Foot technique.
3. Coordination.
4. Applying them to various musical styles.

This is also how this manual is structured.

The fundamentals of hand technique are called the rudiments — the basic elements of playing using your hands — single and double strokes, flams and combinations of all the above.

I would like to draw your attention to the fact that this is a beginner's guide, and, in a sense, an overview. I would recommend finding additional study material. Regarding the above-mentioned topic of rudiments, I'd advise you to buy and study the book "Stick Control" by George Lawrence Stone. It focuses solely on the rudiments. The book is fundamental in the area of rudiments and hand technique development.

Similarly, to help you further with coordination, I would recommend two books as additional study material. The first is Jim Chapin's "Advanced Techniques for the Modern Drummer", a textbook first published in 1948 but still relevant to this day. This book deals mainly with coordination in the jazz and swing style. The second coordination book I would recommend is Harry Chester's "New Breed", a seminal work on coordination when playing drums in a more modern funk style.

Mastering this additional literature will give you more control in playing the drum kit.

Tips for practicing
1. Exercises and the mastery of new techniques involve the use and reprogramming of muscle memory. You should start with the slowest possible tempo, using a metronome.

As strange as it may seem, practicing at a slow pace speeds up the learning process. Also, this way you will not have to undo the damage done by learning the wrong way.

2. Use a mirror when practicing.

This way you become both a teacher and a student at the same time. These lessons will help you see from the outside all the errors in your hand technique, staging of the stroke and in your posture at the instrument.

3. Use a clock or timer.

I recommend spending at least 5 minutes on each exercise.

4. Use a metronome.

The metronome helps you develop an "internal clock" so you become a rhythm carrier, a generator. The metronome will also help you track your tempo progress.

5. Use audio and video recording.

Record yourself on video or voice recorder. This will give you an objective feedback as you will be able to hear yourself play.

Andrey Pankratov

Hand Placement. Grip

The grip is the way we hold the stick. There are several basic types of grips used when playing a drum kit.

In my opinion, the basic grip is the matching German Grip, which comes from the German classical orchestral school.

Video 1

Both hands hold the stick the same way, symmetrically.

The wrists face upwards, the stick is gripped and held with the thumb and middle finger, with the index finger as a guide. The other fingers gently grasp the stick. Here the important this is to find the right balance of the stick in your hand.

Also, you should not grip the stick too tightly, otherwise the bounce will be impossible and your arm muscles will clench.

The German grip involves more of the wrist and the forearm.

This is a fairly universal grip, it is used by classical musicians, jazz musicians and rock players.

In my opinion, the German symmetrical grip is where you should start your training.

An alternative to the German is the French matching grip.

This grip is more suited for finger playing and for rolls with single strokes without accents. The thumbs face upwards, the hands are turned towards each other.

French Grip comes to us from classical timpani playing technique. I would recommend starting to learn the French Grip after mastering the German Grip. In any case, try to hold the stick lightly, don't clutch at it.

Hold the stick lightly enough to prevent it from falling out of your hands.

French Grip

Matched Grip

Traditional Grip

Matched Grip Fulcrum Analysis

Notation. Beat or Measure

Drums, cymbals and the parts of drum set are percussion instruments with indefinite pitch (unlike xylophone, timpani, vibraphone or marimba), so their musical notation by pitch is conventional: each drum is assigned a certain line on the staff, cymbals and hi-hat are written using a note with a cross. It means that the most important thing in drum notation is rhythm, not the pitch.

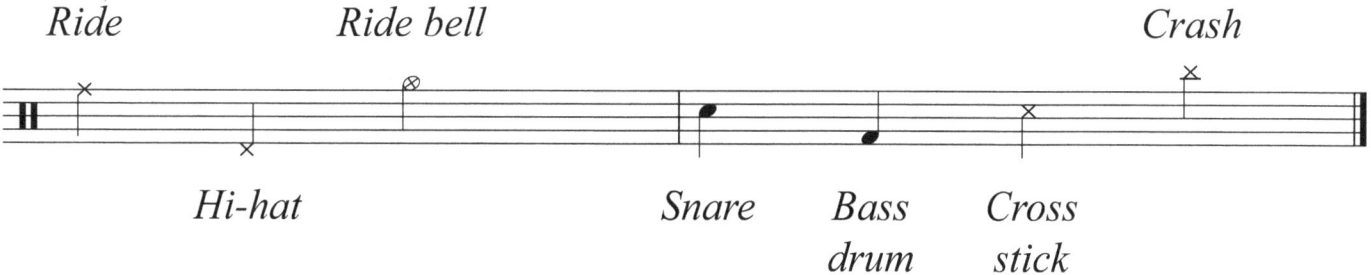

Here are the main types of durations:

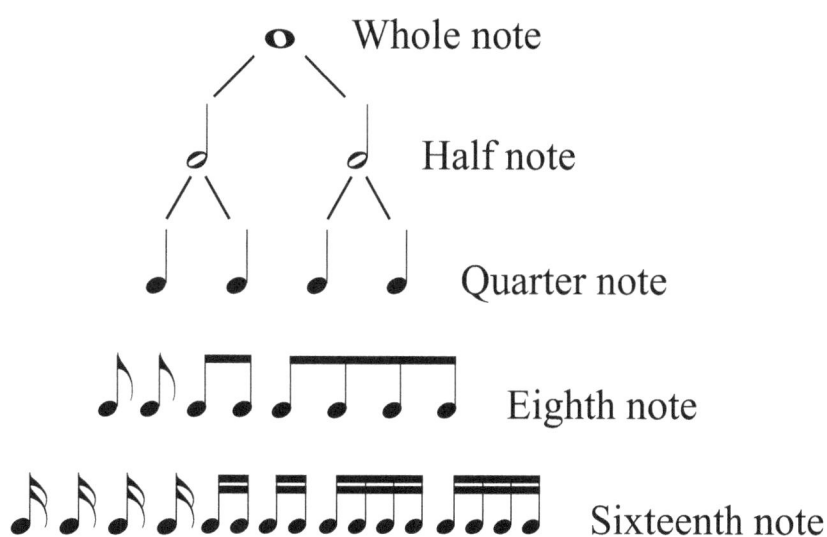

Here are the main rests:

𝄻	Full rest =	𝅝
𝄼	Half rest =	𝅗𝅥
𝄽	Quarter rest =	♩
𝄾	Eighth rest =	♪
𝄿	Sixteenth rest =	𝅘𝅥𝅯

Time Signatures

In musical notation, a measure (or a bar) is a set of notes and rests enclosed between two bar lines — vertical lines crossing the musical staff.

The bar line is placed before the first beat of the measure.

Each measure has a "time" — the number of rhythmic units in a measure, which is written as a fraction: 4/4, 7/8, 11/16, etc.

The 2/4, 3/4, 4/4 Time Signatures

When practicing drums, it is important to learn to count aloud the number of beats in a given measure being played at the moment. This is also a kind of coordination work.

The voice acts as a fifth element, in addition to the arms and legs.

The 3/4 Time Signature

This three-beat measure is quite common in classical and modern European music. It is best known as the dance and musical style called the Waltz.

In the waltz, within one measure, the harmony does not change. This creates the characteristic features of the accompaniment with an emphasis on the downbeat in the bass and two identical chords on the two off-beat beats. This feature is also reflected in the rhythm of the percussion.

Example of the Waltz or 3/4 time signature

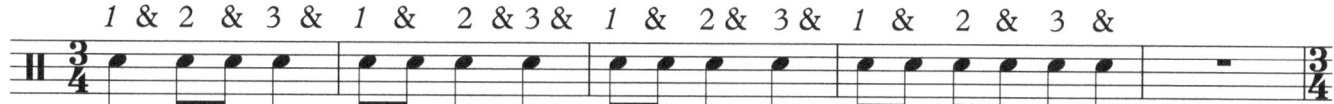

Example of Bolero

Example of the 3/4 time signature

The 4/4 Time Signature

The 4/4 measure is probably the most popular measure in European and American music.

Jazz, rock-and-roll, disco, rock, pop — countless pieces of music have been written in this time signature.

Most of the examples in this book are also in the 4/4 time signature.

"Hand to Hand" Technique

One of the most important, basic principles of drumming is a technique called "Hand to hand" — alternating your hands while playing.

It means that you always start playing the downbeat with your lead hand (in this case, as an illustration, the right hand).

The left hand follows the right hand. This is how you play the snare drum.

Eventually, you transfer this concept to playing the entire drum kit.

The lead hand starts the beat, keeps the rhythm on the ride cymbal or hi-hat, serving like an anchor and starting point of counting.

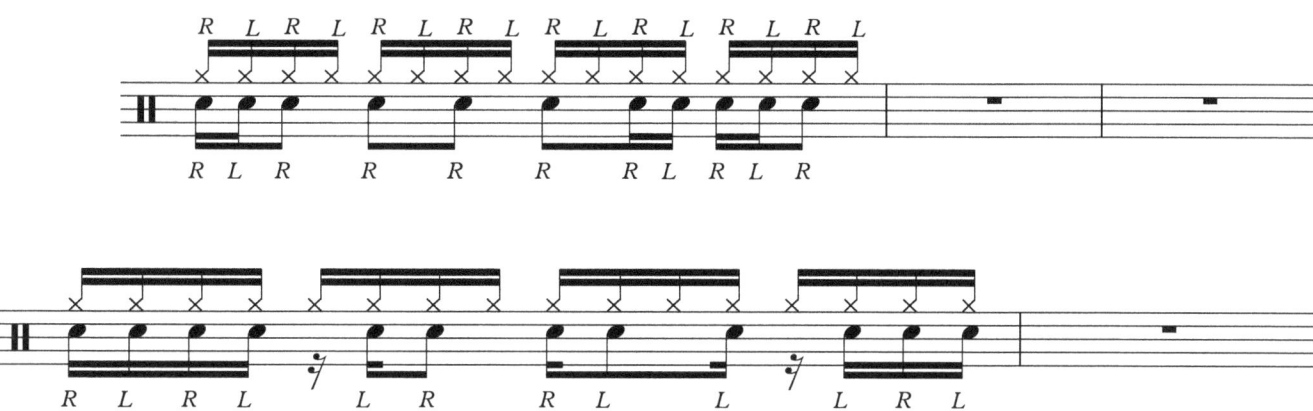

The hands alternate as if you were playing a constant pulse using sixteenth notes.

The quarters and eighths go to the right hand, while the off-beat 16-ths go to the left hand.

This is not the only correct way to play, but it makes it easier to understand the logic of alternating hands (stickings) behind the drum kit when playing beats and fill-ins.

Kick, Snare, Hat

The bass drum, snare and hi-hat are the percussion instruments together make up the foundation for a steady rhythm in modern music.

That's why it's so important to start with the basics. These three instruments fill in the spectrum of low, mid, and high frequencies.

The bass drum creates the foundation of the groove, the snare creates movement by emphasizing different parts of the beat (like the 2nd and 4th), and the hi-hat creates and maintains the rhythmic pulsation, much like a shaker in percussion.

Together they form a complete rhythmic pattern, or groove.

In fact, this is how they should be perceived — as a single instrument.

Types of Strokes. Full Stroke

When playing drums, different strokes and their combinations are used to achieve different dynamic effects.

The Full Stroke is a stroke with maximum amplitude.

The elbow goes to the side and upwards, the stick is held easily and sags, then the elbow goes downwards, then a whiplike, powerful stroke follows, then you put the stick in the initial position about 1–1½ inches from the surface of the snare drum.

I recommend practicing this type of beat separately on the pad at an extremely slow tempo so you can work out all the elements of the movement and achieve smoothness. The tempo is 40 beats per minute (bpm).

Video 2   *Video 3*   *Video 4*

Types of Strokes. Moeller Technique

Sanford Moeller (1880–1960) was an American drum teacher and performer. In the early twentieth century he studied the performance technique of many U.S. Civil War marching drummers who, even at an advanced age, were able to play fast and powerful.

As a result, he formulated the principles of basic technique for playing accented and unaccented beats. These principles became the basis for teaching drumming technique and also bear his name.

In a nutshell, the essence of this technique is that when you make a downstroke, you use the energy of that downstroke to perform subsequent unaccented strokes. That is, the energy of one downstroke is enough for several following strokes, which are performed automatically, without additional effort.

For the accented Stroke you use the same whip-like motion as in the full stroke. It is important to keep in mind that the force of the stroke is generated by the weight of the stick and the length of its trajectory, not by muscle tension.
As a result, there are several types of strokes that are inextricably linked between them.

The Moeller Stroke is an accentuated, powerful stroke that comes in three variants, depending on the necessary playing dynamics:
1. High Moeller — a stroke with maximum amplitude (Full Stroke) — from the shoulder.
2. Medium Moeller — medium amplitude, elbow stroke is used.
3. Low Moeller — minimal amplitude, mainly involving the wrist.
The downstroke in this technique allows us to execute the following non-accented kicks called taps.

Make a tap and let the stick bounce back making a certain number of taps. This way, the Tap follows the Downstroke. The third type of tap is the Upstroke, which is a stroke in a series of strokes that precedes the Downstroke, i.e. the accented beat.

Unlike Downstroke and Tap, Upstroke does not exist on its own, separate from the series. In fact, it is a Tap stroke, which, going up, precedes the Downstroke blow.

In other words, the essence of Moeller's technique is revealed primarily when playing a series of strokes.

The Moeller's technique and three types of strokes:

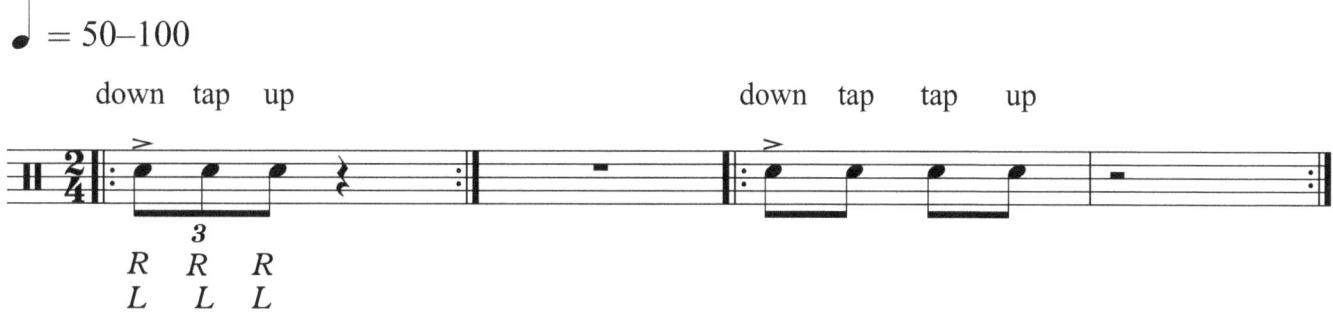

Options: 1. Left hand. 2. Right hand. 3. Both together.

To summarize — the above technique is used when playing most of the accented rudiments that will be discussed in this manual.

Exercises for the development of the Upstroke:

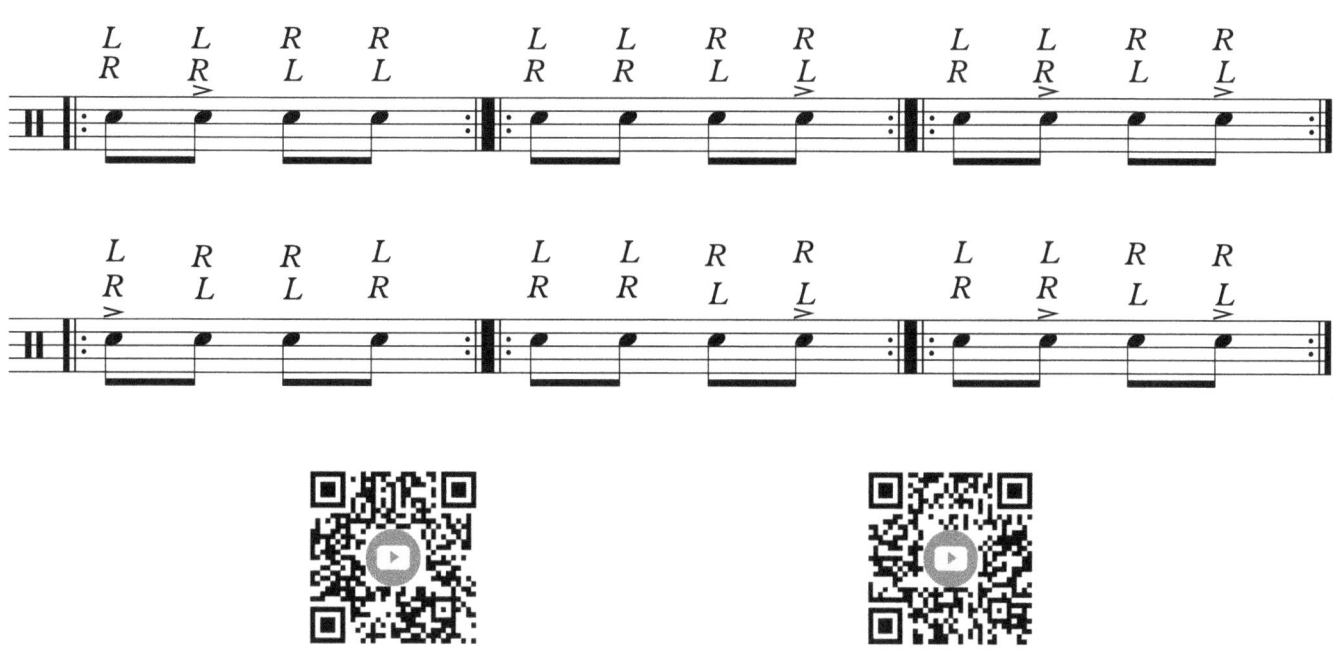

Video 6 *Video 7*

17

In triplet pulsation

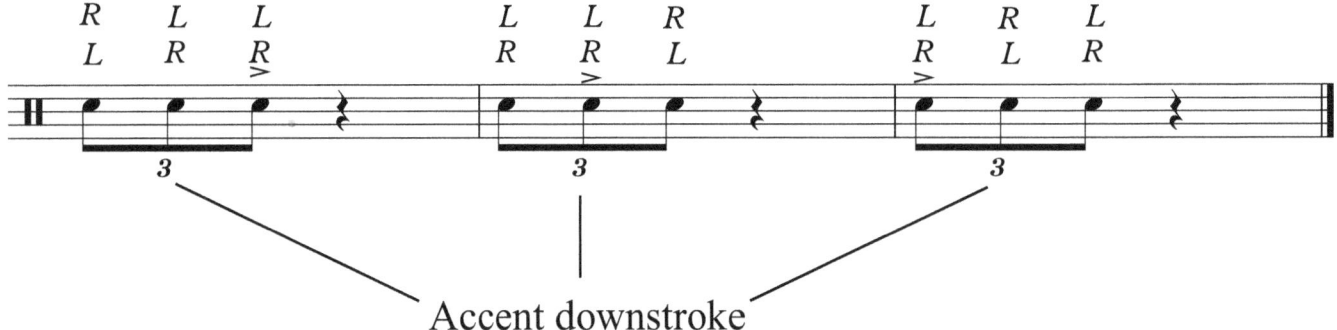

Triplets

A triplet is a group of three notes of the same duration, equal in time to two notes of the same duration.

Triplet durations:

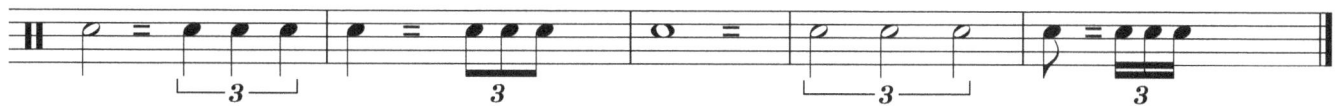

The video example demonstrates the performance of eighth-note triplets.
Note that the Moeller technique is used when performing triplets with emphasis on each downbeat.

Accents are played as Downstroke, unaccented strokes are played as Tap.

Video 5

Playing Single Strokes and Accents

Single strokes – when you alternate between the left and right hands – are probably the most basic element of drumming.

The dynamic emphasis of a particular beat is called an accent.

Example:

Playing sixteenth notes, the quarters are emphasized:

By combining variations of accents, you can create different rhythmic textures:

Video 7 1

Rudiments

Rudiments are the basic elements of playing, stickings, and are an essential component of developing drumstick control skills.

Rudiments are essentially the ABC's and syllables of the drumming language. Single and Double Strokes are also considered Rudiments.

Further on are their derivatives, combinations of Single and Double Strokes called the Paradiddles.

Triple paradiddle

Start at ♩ = 50–100

Video 8

All of these rudiments should be practiced separately for at least five minutes each without stopping.

Start at a tempo of 60 bpm.

I highly recommend the book "Stick Control" by George Lawrence Stone, where you will find a lot of exercises to work on most of the known rudiments in more detail.

Simon Phillips Exercise
2 singles + 2 doubles + 2 triples

Play for around 5 minutes.

Flam

The Flam (or grace note, also known as *Vorschlag* in German from *vor* — "before" and *Schlag* — "beat") is an additional, quieter beat that precedes the main accent and, in fact, strengthens it, giving an additional volume to the sound.

There are single, double, triple, and four-note flams.

In musical notation, a single flam is written with a small crossed out eighth note; a double, triple, and other flams are written with small 16th notes.

Single flam

Double flam

Triple flam

Four-note flam

Exercise

Video 9

Video 10

Flam Accent

Let's continue to learn about the flams. One of the most important flam rudiments is the flam accent.

A flam accent is a triplet with a flam that falls on the third beat of the triplet:

Let's look at it using slow tempo of 60 bpm.

Combine a single paradiddle with a single flam on each downbeat to create a rudiment called a flam paradiddle:

Flam double paradiddle:

Note that here you get three strokes in a row with each hand alternating!
This is a good exercise to develop technique and warm up your hands before a performance.

The flam tap is a rudiment that combines double strokes and single flams on each downbeat:

Practice this element separately, starting at a slow tempo, and then combine it with flam paradiddle in the same exercise:

Video 9 1

Video 11

All Videos (Playlist)

All videos are included in the same playlist on YouTube *(online)*:

or use the link:

cutt.ly/HrXcktoL

Short Rolls

Short Rolls are double-stroke rolls that consist of a series of double strokes of varying lengths followed by an emphasis on the downbeat.

The most common and frequently used are five-stroke rolls, seven-stroke rolls, and nine-stroke rolls, which you will learn about below:

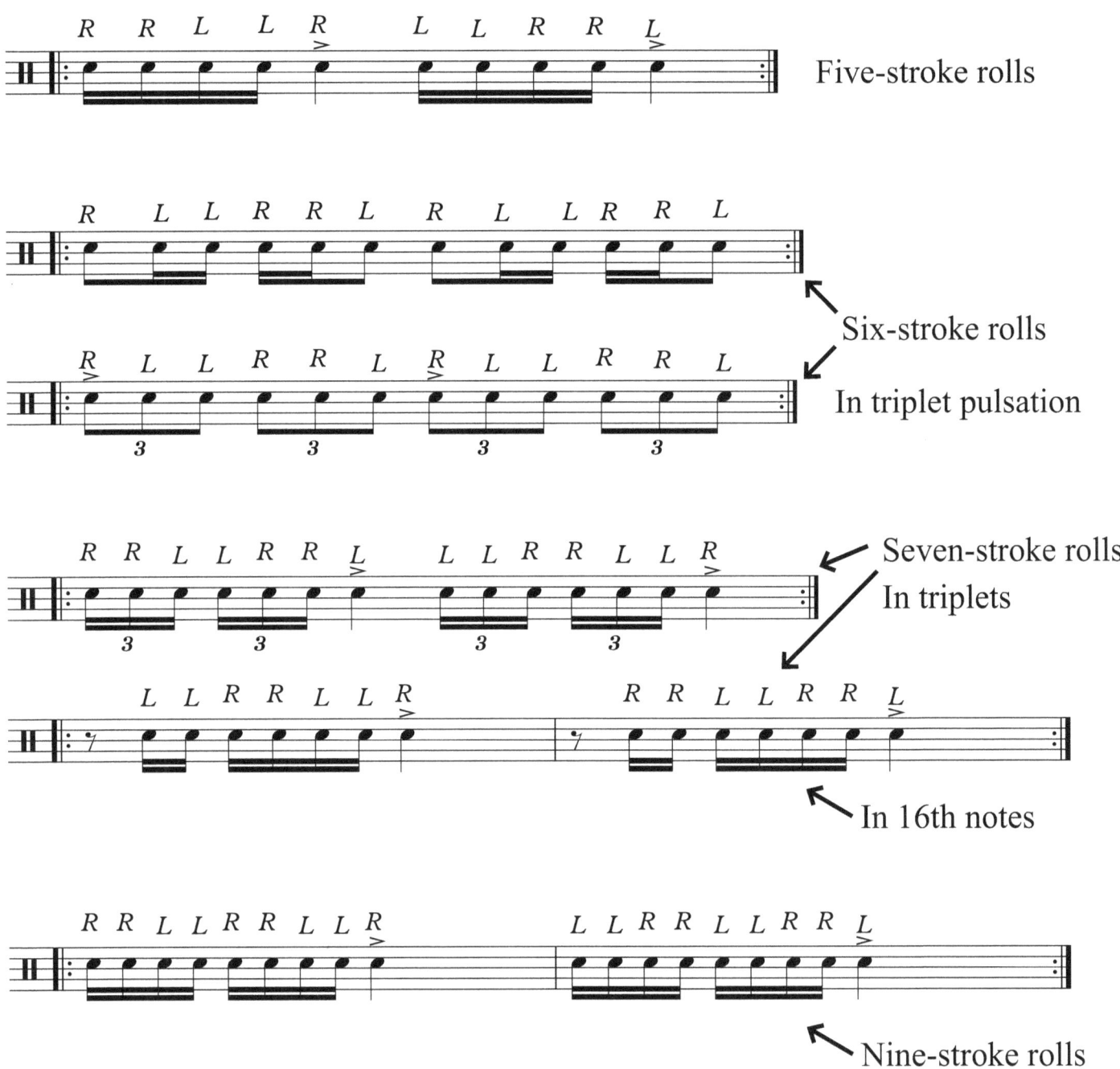

Exercise for short fractions

R L R L R R L L R R L L R L R L R R L L R R L L

Nine-stroke rolls

L R L R L L R L L R R   L R L R   L L R R   L L R R
R R L L R R L L R R L L   R R L L   R R L L R R L L
L L R R L L R R L L R R   L L R R   L L R R L L R R

R R L L R   L L R R L   R R L L   R

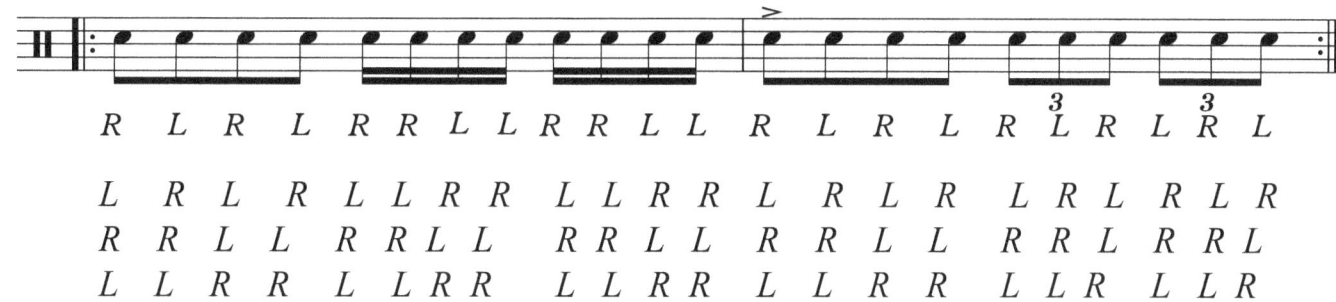

R L R L R R L L R R L L R L R L R L R L R L R L
                                                                                                  3   3

L R L R L L R R   L L R R L R L R   L R L R L R
R R L L R R L L   R R L L R R L L   R R L R R L
L L R R L L R R   L L R R L L R R   L L R L L R

Video 12

Video 13

Crazy Army sheet music

Pedal Drumming. Playing the Bass Drum

There are several different basic techniques for playing the bass drum (often called the kick drum).

Originally (historically), it all started with a technique called Heel Down, which is when the sole of the foot rests against the pedal platform.

Video 14

This technique is still used today, mostly in jazz and lighter styles for more delicate style of playing.

One of the advantages of this technique is that you can practice anywhere, and you don't actually need pedals to do it. Just sit down and try playing even quarters with your right foot on the floor.

Over time, you can try to add your hands.

Try to repeat the same rhythmic patterns that you play with your hands.

The tempo of the metronome is slow — start at 60 bpm.

Play different rudiments with your hands and at the same time play quarter notes with your right foot.

Try to play so that your foot and hands match perfectly, avoiding involuntary "flams" between your hands and feet.

An alternative to this technique is the Heel Up technique, i.e. when the weight of the foot is transferred to the toe, the heel hangs in the air, and the beater is pressed against the surface of the plastic of the drum.

This technique allows you to achieve a more powerful sound production.

It is used in rock and also in other genres that require a more powerful sound.

Here is an exercise to develop speed and control of the bass drum.

Play a measure using sixteenth notes, a measure of eighths, and a measure of 8 triplets.

Repeat again, playing at a more moderate pace, practicing for at least five minutes without stopping:

Subsequently, add quarters in the left foot on the hi-hat.

Next, play the same exercise on the hi-hat pedal, playing quarters on the bass drum.

Bass drum exercises

Video 15

Jumping a bit ahead, I would like to offer you one more exercise for bass drum, which also develops coordination skills.

This is a kind of "ladder", as in athletic exercises.

Start with two strokes on the bass drum, add one stroke for each beat, go up to five and then back to two.

On the hi-hat, play sixteenths by hand, snare drum is played on second and fourth beat.

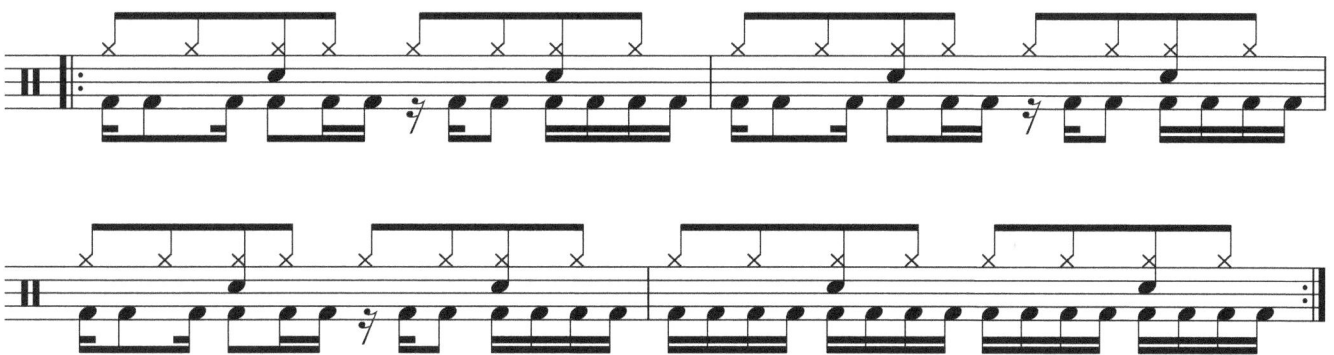

Developing Movement Coordination on the Drum Kit

Coordination of movements between the drummer's hands and feet is the most important element of performance skills. The key to developing coordination and independence is to perform a repetitive part (*ostinato*) using one or more limbs while working on playing various rhythmic variations on the bass drum and/or snare drum with your left hand (if you are right-handed).

You can start with quarter and/or eighth notes in the right or left hand (if you are left-handed) — this will be your first *ostinato*.

The other hand will play different variations using quarters, eighths, sixteenths, triplets, and combinations of different rhythmic patterns.

In this way, step by step, you will work through all possible rhythmic variations while achieving a certain freedom in rhythmic improvisation.

Here I would like to recommend two textbooks dedicated exclusively to coordination behind the drums. These are "New Breed" by Harry Chester and "Advanced Studies for the Modern Drummer" by Jim Chapin. You can also find a list of recommended literature for further study included at the end of this book.

Below I would like to offer you some simple *ostinatos* to develop basic coordination.

Begin by leading with your strong hand — your right hand if you are right-handed.

Then I'll give you a rhythmic text, various patterns, which you will have to play with your right foot on the bass drum, or with your left hand on the snare drum, if the bass drum is already present in the *ostinato*.

Ride cymbal
Share drum
Bass drum plays rhythms from sec. 2

Add quarter note hi-hat with foot

Share plays rhythms from sec. 2

The following are the patterns to be performed on the snare drum with the left hand, or on the bass drum or hi-hat pedal with the left foot.

Each measure of the pattern is worked out separately along with a selected *ostinato* from those listed above.

Section 2

Rhythms in sec. 2 are to be played with *ostinatos* (on share or buss drum).

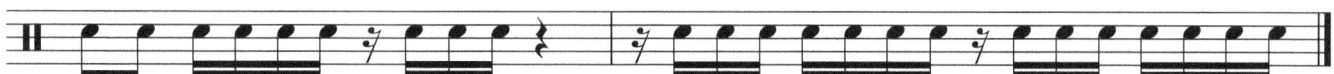

Video 16

Video 17

Coordination in Triplet Pulsation in Swing Style

The next step in the development of coordination is to work on the triplet pulsation in the jazz, swing style.

In this case I'd strongly recommend the "Advanced Techniques for the Modern Drummer" by American drummer and educator Jim Chapin.

This truly fundamental work was first published in 1948, has been reprinted many times and has not lost its relevance to this day.

What is the essence of this type of rhythms?

Earlier you learned about the pulsation of ordinary eighths or sixteenths. Now it is the triplet pulsation.

This means that everything you play here one way or another will coincide with a constant triplet rhythm.

The word "swing" itself means "swaying", that is, the regular eighths turn into a triplet with a missing second beat. The ear perceives the regular eighths as if they are distorted and swing.

straight eights → swing feel

By the way, this rhythm has its own name: "shuffle". It is a separate rhythmic style in music. You will learn about it later.

Going back to swing, it should be noted that traditionally scores in this style are written in eighths, but with the note "a swing feel". This means that they should be performed in triplet pulse, as shown in the example above.

The basis of the swing rhythm is the *ostinato*, which is played on the ride cymbal and hi-hat.

It looks as follows:

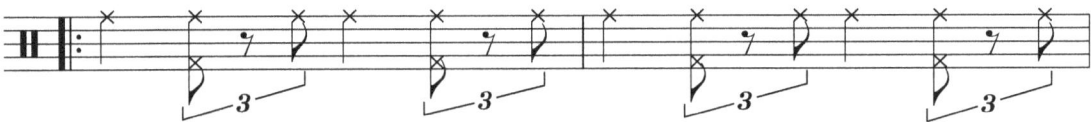

It can also be written as:

Video 18

Or as follows:

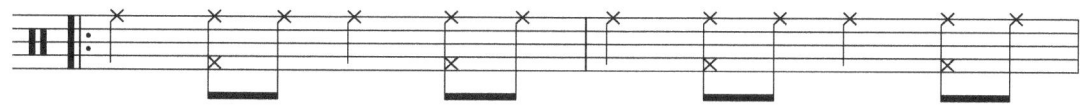

In each case, it will sound the same. Different variants of notation are there for convenience.

Video 18 1

Here you have the same task as in the previous section: to work through all possible rhythmic combinations in the left hand on the snare drum, then in the right foot on the bass drum, the left foot on the hi-hat, and then — combinations of snare and snare drum with the addition of variations in the left foot using the hi-hat.

Start, as usual, with simple patterns in the left hand. The snare drum can add soft quarters using the "flat foot" technique described in the "Pedal Playing" section above.

Again, these quarters should sound soft, as they say, "felt but not heard".

Below are several variations of rhythms to be played with the left hand on the snare drum and a combination of snare and bass drums. All of these are performed against the backdrop of the swing rhythm on the ride cymbal and hi-hat for the second and fourth beats.

Be sure to get Jim Chapin's book where you will find a great number of variations of these kinds of rhythms. As you work through them, you will get the necessary freedom on the way to mastering jazz improvisation.

An alternative variation of *ostinato* would be to play shuffle on the cymbal.

 Play shuffle on the ride cymbal

Rhythmic variations are to be played on snare, bass drum, or hi-hat with foot.

Solo combinations are to be played with the left hand on the snare drum and with the right foot on the bass drum; snare + kick combinations, with hi-hat on 2 & 4, are to be played with the foot.

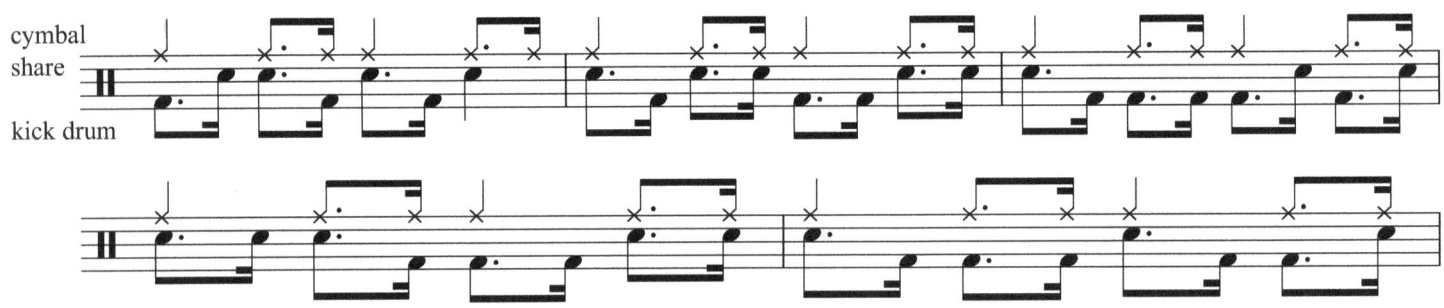

16 notes & triplets

Linear Coordination

Linear playing and linear rhythmic pattern mean that the strokes are played sequentially, one after the other. They never sound at the same time and never overlap. In music it is also called monophony.

Obviously, this type of coordination is radically different from what you learned in the previous chapters about a basic, repetitive part (*ostinato*), the pattern on which the rhythm was built.

There are a number of basic exercises for developing linear type coordination.

Play 1/4 notes hi-hat with foot.

The exercises should be performed with the bass drum, then the hi-hat, then add the hi-hat with quarter notes and eighths, played with the left foot.

This way, these exercises will provide the necessary technical foundation for performing variations in breaks and linear rhythmic patterns.

Linear grooves

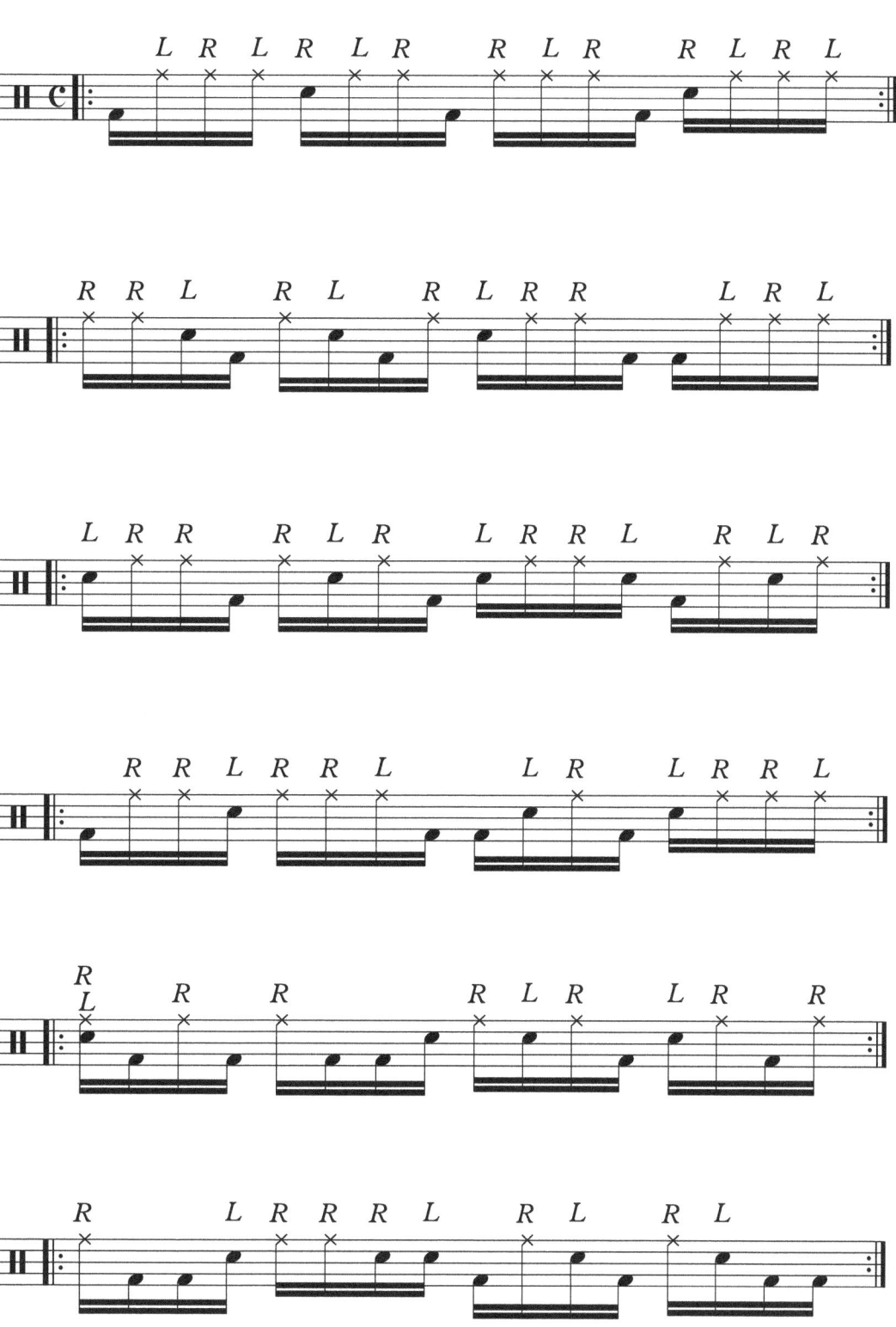

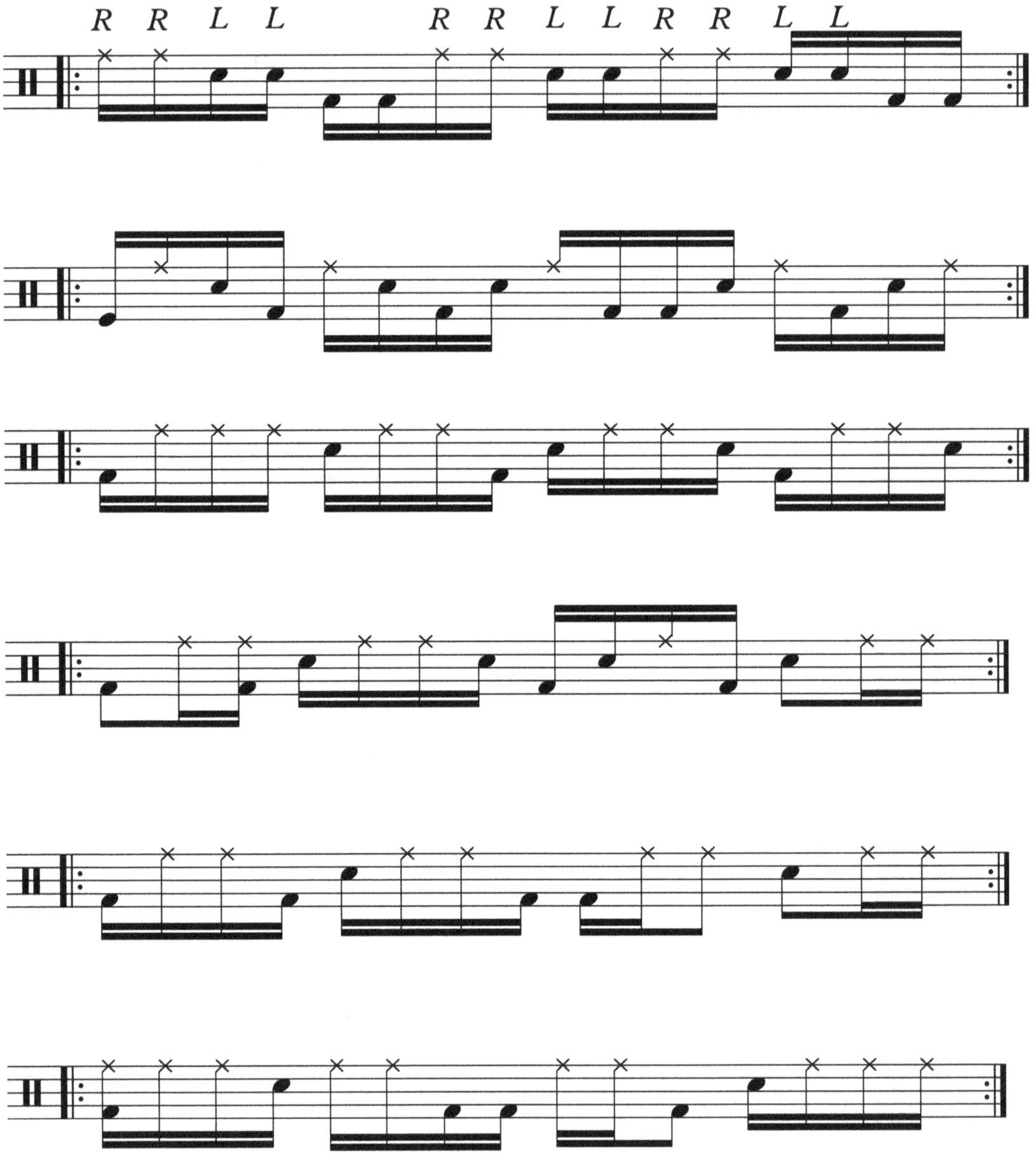

Video 19

Music Styles

As a nice and informative bonus to this manual, I would like to offer you my review of some musical styles and their respective rhythmic patterns. This review is by no means intended to be comprehensive, but rather a small sampling of the styles that have served as the foundation of modern pop and rock music. Additionally, practicing these rhythms will build the necessary knowledge and serve as good coordination and rhythmic practice.

Jazz

Historically, jazz was the first musical style where an instrument called the drumset was formed and truly shined.

Indeed, the history of jazz music is inextricably linked to such truly great names as Gene Krupa, Buddy Rich, Art Blakey, Elvin Jones and others.

The music played by American big bands of the 30's and 40's demanded more from the drummer than just keeping the beat.

If you listen carefully to the masters of the style, you will hear not only perfect swing, but also an understanding of harmonic form, support of the soloist's melodies, variation of the accompaniment, and logical construction of solos.

For a complete immersion in the study of this style I recommend "The Art of Bop Drumming" and "Beyond Bop" by John Riley, which are fully devoted to jazz drumming.

The rhythmic basis of most jazz music is a rhythm called "swing". In fact, you have already had the pleasure of learning about it above in the "Coordination" section of this manual.

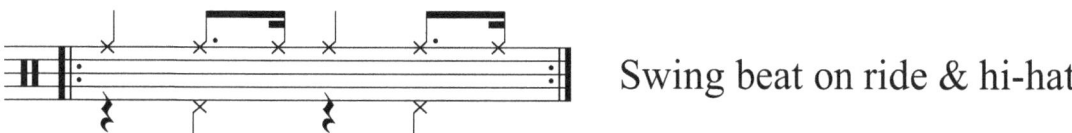 Swing beat on ride & hi-hat

This is swing. The cymbal creates a quarter-note rhythm that pulsates with the eighth triplets. The hi-hat emphasizes the 2nd and 4th beats, creating a forward motion. This is the foundation of the jazz beat.

Note that to emphasize the second and fourth beats, you need a clear idea of where the downbeat is.

In general, the accent on 2 and 4 is what rhythmically unites these seemingly distant styles — jazz and rock.

Against the background of a constant swinging pulse in the cymbal and hi-hat, the snare and bass drum improvise, emphasizing the changing syncopated texture of the melody or "dialoguing" with the soloist.

In this way, the rhythm becomes highly variable, "alive", but at the same time in constant forward motion. That is why the name of the cymbal is "ride" — recalling driving movement.

Shuffle

Next in line — in a sense, a derivative of swing, a special case, so to speak, a rhythm called shuffle.

This rhythm is mostly used in the blues style.

Blues is a style of African-American music that originated in the mid-nineteenth century among cotton plantation laborers, so a blues song is essentially a work song. The blues has influenced many musical styles — pop, jazz, rock and roll, soul — all of which drew their inspiration from it. Most blues songs have a 12 bar form.

The shuffle rhythm is the basis for most blues compositions.

Double shuffle on snare & ride quarter notes on B. D. 2 & 4 on hi-hat

There are many variations of the shuffle. The one above is called "Double shuffle" — double because both hands play the shuffle at the same time. Alternatively, you can play swing on the cymbal, which will make the texture a little easier.

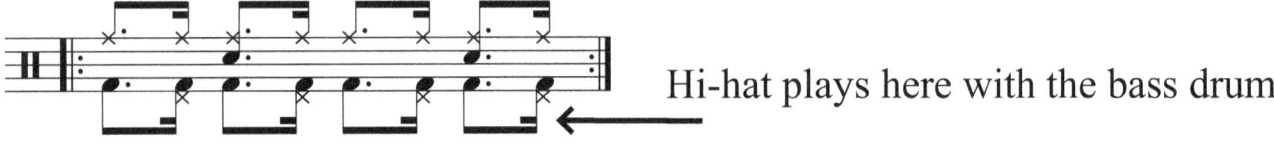

Hi-hat plays here with the bass drum

You can also play the shuffle on the bass drum, while playing with your foot on the hi-hat on the 3rd beat of the triplet. This pattern in itself will serve as a coordination challenge!

Rock'n'Roll

Another music style and rhythm that has become classic is rock'n'roll.

In terms of musical form, it is similar to the blues, the same 12-stroke form, the same harmony, but the rhythm is radically different.

This rhythm is quite simple, but very useful in developing your single strokes.

You will be playing eighth notes on the snare drum with the rim shot accent on the 2 and 4 beats, the semi-open hi-hat repeats the snare drum part, also playing eighth notes. The bass drum can play either quarter notes or a random pattern of eighth notes.

 Hi-hat is half open

The hands play synchronized eighths with accents, so this rhythm in itself is an excellent exercise for working on your single strokes using the Moeller technique.

Some of you might remember the famous "Rock'n'Roll" song by Led Zeppelin and the drum intro by John Bonham:

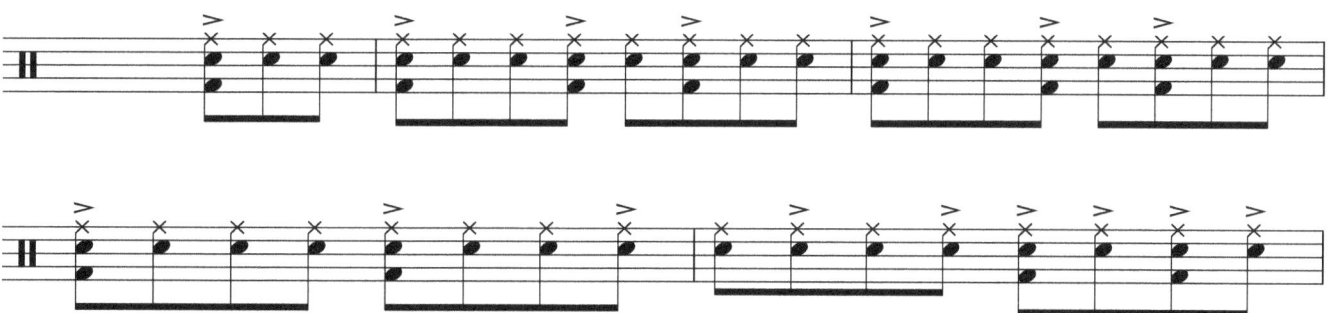

In this intro, the drums come in from behind the beat, sort of mimicking the guitar intro of another famous classic rock'n'roll piece, "Johnny B Goode"

This piece is a great illustration of the whole style.

Funk and soul

Another musical style that has served as the rhythmic basis for most pop music of the last decades is funk.

Funk is an African-American style. You might say it is a heavier version of rhythm and blues that has originated in the 1960s in the United States. Funk is dance music characterized by heavy syncopation, pulsating rhythm, harmonic minimalism and meditative repetitive rhythmic phrases.

I recommend diving into the history and getting to know the works of James Brown, George Clinton, Sly and the Family Stone, Cool and the Gang and others.

I would like to emphasize one important detail — a feature that unites all styles of American music is the emphasis on the 2nd and 4th beats. This feature is called "Backbeat". It creates the perception of a constant forward movement. The music doesn't linger. To one degree or another, the backbeat is present in all of these styles and is their foundation.

The basic funk rhythm, sometimes jokingly called "Money Beat", is no exception.

I'm guessing that it is called the Money Beat because these are, you might say, the basics. Once you have mastered them, you can become part of the world of show biz pros. (But that's just my guess.)

All joking aside, for many folks, this is the first beat that starts them on the road to learning drums. If you'd like, you could diversify this rhythm with ghost notes ('ghost notes' are quiet 'tap' strokes), which will fill the void without changing the structure of the rhythm, adding pulsating sixteenth notes.

Snare notes in parantheses are ghost notes to be played softly

A few classic funky beats you must know:

James Brown's "Funky Drummer"

Herbie Hancock's "Chameleon"

44

This is another interesting beat. Here the hands play sixteenths on the hi-hat with the emphasis on the 2 and 4 on the snare drum. Here, as an illustration, is an example from Michael Jackson's work, the composition 'Wanna Be Starting Something' with Jonathan Moffett on drums:

This beat is a great exercise in itself. It's an opportunity to work through the technique of single strokes in the hands and doubles on the bass drum.

Disco rhythm is the same single sixteenths strokes on hi-hat, 2s and 4s on snare drum and quarters on the bass drum:

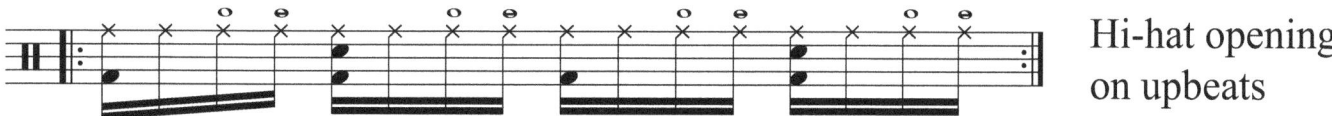

Hi-hat opening on upbeats

Video 20

A Couple More Funk Drawings

A funk classic and an example of linear groove from the late 60's. American band The Meters and their song "Cissy Strut":

Video 21

James Brown's "Cold Sweat" is an example of an interesting shift of the snare drum to an off-beat eighth:

In the video, this example is played by me in improvisational manner, with sixteenth note variations.

Another iconic funk groove I'd like to explore is a rhythm called the funk shuffle. Sometimes it is also called the 'Purdie shuffle' after the legendary living drummer Bernard 'Pretty' Purdie:

What makes this pattern special is that it combines swing, triplet pulsation layered on top of a funk beat.
The ghost notes make this beat seem three-dimensional.

Brazilian and Afro-Cuban Rhythms

Bossa Nova

Bossa Nova is a style of Brazilian jazz music that emerged in the 1950s. In terms of rhythm, it is essentially a slowed down and delicately played samba.

Eighth notes can be played on the hi-hat, ride cymbal or brushed on the snare drum.

The constant rhythm of the bass drum and hi-hat form an *ostinato*, which can be used to work on your coordination and independence of the left hand by playing the variation patterns from Harry Chester's "New Breed" book.

I also recommend to you Maria Martinez's "Brazilian Coordination for the Drumset" — a book that addressed the issue of coordination in Brazilian rhythms.

Samba

Samba is a Brazilian musical genre of African origin, combining music and dance. In a carnival procession, there are many performers that play a variety of percussion instruments and, by transposing these rhythms to the drum kit, the drummer has to stand in for several performers all alone.

The rhythm 'samba' is more mobile and driven.

The pattern of the bass drum is the same as in bossa nova. It copies the rhythm of folk drums "surdo". The bass variation of the pandeiro drum rhythm is played on the snare drum and looks as follows:

Basic samba beat on snare

All right hand strokes are played accented, the left hand part can be moved to a closed hi-hat.

Here is a slightly more complicated version with a ride cymbal:

Ride cymbal
Snare drum
Bass drum & hi-hat with foot

This is more like a jazz samba, with the variation of rhythm in the left hand being an important element, so it is worth taking the time to develop coordination and independence within this pattern.

In all of the above patterns, you will be playing eight note off-beats or all eighth notes in a measure on the hi-hat with the left foot.

Ride cymbal
Snare
Floor tom
Bass drum

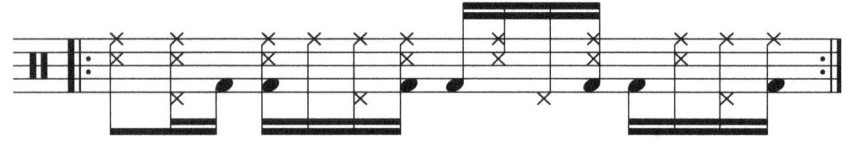

Cross stick on snare drum

Baiao (Bayon)

Bayon is another interesting Brazilian rhythm.
It is also an *ostinato* on the bass drum.

And this is what the whole pattern looks like:

Variations:

Cymbal bell
Snare
Bass drum & hi-hat
With foot

Salsa, Afro-Cuban rhythms

Just as jazz, pop and funk grooves are based on the backbeat (2 and 4 beats), Afro-Cuban music is based on the "clave" pattern.

Clave is a two-measure pattern played with two sticks called claves (hence the pattern name).

Clave can be 2:3 or 3:2, depending on which of the two measures is played first.

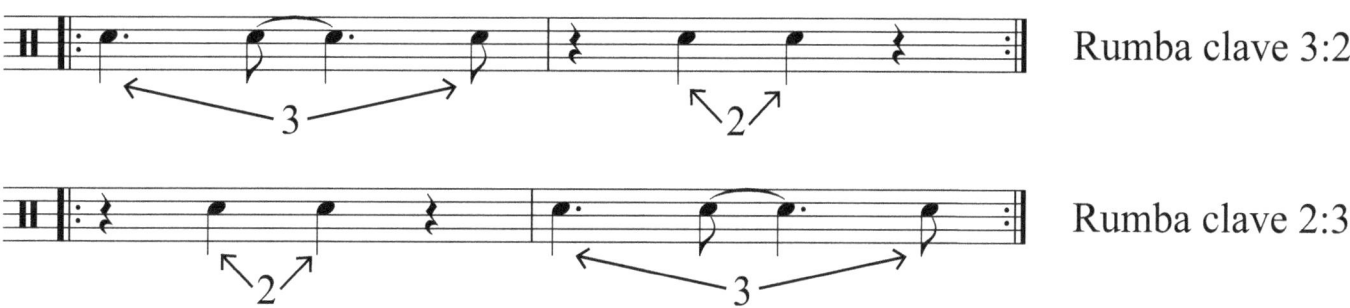

Rumba clave 3:2

Rumba clave 2:3

To summarize, in jazz or pop music, you clap or snap your fingers on 2 and on 4, but in salsa you play clave rhythm.

On a drum kit, clave rhythm can be played on the rim of the snare drum. On the hi-hat, or ride cymbal, a rhythm called cascara is played, and the rhythm of the bass drum is called tumbao:

Cascara beat

Tumbao beat
Bass drum

Together it looks like this:

All parts together

Cowbell variation:

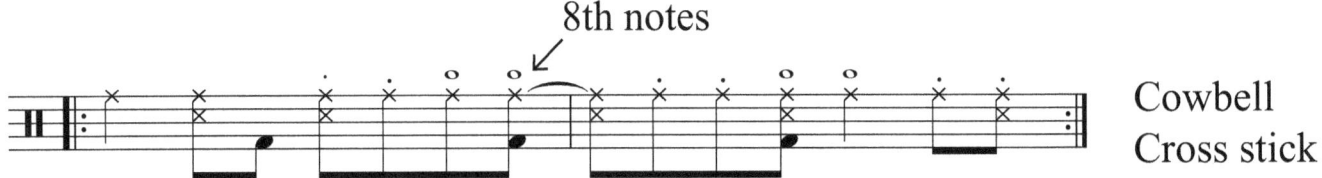

Cowbell
Cross stick

Cowbell plus snare drum:

Songo

Songo is a rhythm created especially for the drum kit by the famous percussionist Jose Quintana in the 1970s. This rhythm is often used in Afro-Cuban jazz and fusion music.

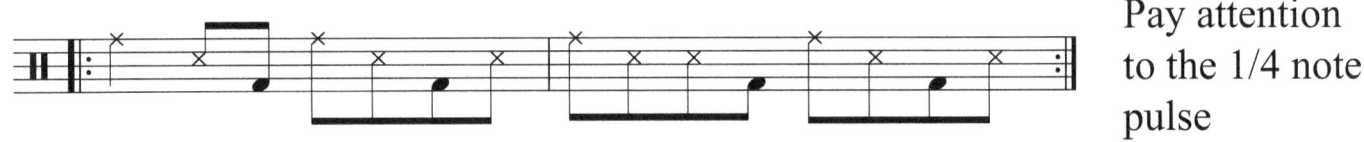

Pay attention to the 1/4 note pulse

Bembe. Afro-Cuban 6/8

This rhythm has African roots and it is played in triplet pulsation in the 6/8 time signature.

Note that the clave rhythm can be traced in this time signature as well, but it is modified, as if "stretched out" in triplets.

Mozambique

Mozambique is a rhythm that is even more often used in playing rock or funk than in Afro-Cuban music per se. This beat was made famous by the legendary Steve Gadd.

Video 22   *Video 23*

Train Beat

Train beat is a steamroller beat, a 'locomotive' — a country style rhythm. Great for practicing single accented strokes.

It's also suitable for those taking their first steps learning coordination behind the drum kit. The kick drum and hi-hat rhythm here are as simple as they get.

The rhythm is played at a brisk pace, but, as always, start learning at a slow pace. The main thing is the quality of execution.

Video 24

Metronome Lessons

Let me say a few words about playing with a metronome.

Most of the exercises in this book have tempo instructions, which means that they should be played using a metronome. Nowadays, 100% of music is recorded in the studio with a metronome, so you will always have to deal with a metronome one way or another. Actually, the metronome is a great point of reference as it generates the tempo and you have to match it.

Video 25

But the main task is a bit different. The point is that you yourself should become the carrier or keeper of tempo and groove. Metronome helps you develop this most important quality. It serves as a kind of a crutch at first. Therefore, initially it is very important to count quarter notes out loud while playing, and also to sing out loud the smaller pulsations in eighth or 16th notes. The goal is to get you to be able to mentally imagine as fast a pulse as possible. This ability ensures you are always on time.

To develop this ability, you can try to imagine the click not as quarters, but as the other, off-beat beats of a measure.

For starters, pick up the tempo of 120 bpm. Now set the tempo twice as slow — 60 bpm and imagine that the click is played not on the 1st, but on the second and fourth beats of a 4/4 time signature. Now you have the first and third beats in your mind, and the click sounds on 2 and 4. Try to get used to this mode by practicing simple rhythmic patterns such as "Money Beat".

Then you can go further and mentally 'shift' the metronome to off-beat eighths. Triple rhythms in the style of 'swing' can be practiced by imagining the metronome click on the third beat of the triplet. There is a video example of practicing this variant. All these techniques of working with the metronome develop your 'internal clock'. You are ramping up your ability to sense the rhythmic pulsation regardless of whether you are playing something at the moment or not. This is how you become a carrier and generator of both tempo and rhythm.

Good luck!

List of Recommended Literature

1. George Lawrence Stone "Stick Control For The Snare Drummer"

2. Ted Reed "Advanced Steps To Syncopation"

3. Joe Morello "Accents And Rebounds"

4. Jim Chapin "Advanced Techniques For The Modern Drummer"

5. Gary Chester "New Breed"

6. Rick Latham "Advanced Funk Studies"

7. Lincoln Goines & Robby Ameen "Funkifying The Clave — Afro-Cuban Grooves For Bass And Drums"

Learning to play your favorite songs on the piano is easy!

Today the piano is probably the most popular musical instrument in the world. Playing this instrument will give you an unforgettable experience.

The book contains musical theory, practical exercises, and 65 popular songs for adults.

ISBN: 979-8361128570
ASIN: B0BKYHL7PC

United States   **United Kingdom**   **Canada**

Complete saxophone instruction book for beginners. For kids 12+ and adults.

This step-by-step guide is for anyone who wants to master the instrument and learn to play their favorite songs effortlessly. The book is also for those who want to learn to swing, play the blues and practice improvisation.

ISBN: 978-1962612098
ASIN: 1962612090

United States   **United Kingdom**   **Canada**

www.ingramcontent.com/pod-product-compliance
Lightning Source LLC
Chambersburg PA
CBHW081330040426
42453CB00013B/2361